IMAGES
of America

HAVERHILL
MASSACHUSETTS
FROM TOWN TO CITY

Up, Up, and Away! Sewell Ford prepares to mount his big-wheel bicycle. The photographer has carefully noted the name of his subject (Ford), the date (May 17, 1888) and the time of day (12:30 pm). The *City Directory* for 1889 gives Ford's address as 245 Washington Street, where he boarded at the house of John F. Ford. No occupation is listed, and nothing more is known of Sewell Ford.

Cover Image: The Store of J. A. Forrest Jr., at 341 Washington Street, next to the Currier School House. Forrest was a "dealer in Groceries and Provisions." John Forrest, the owner of the store, lived at 46 Grove Street.

IMAGES
of America

HAVERHILL
MASSACHUSETTS
FROM TOWN TO CITY

Patricia Trainor O'Malley

ARCADIA
PUBLISHING

Published by Arcadia Publishing
Charleston, South Carolina

Library of Congress Catalog Card Number: 2006935848

For all general information contact Arcadia Publishing at:
Telephone 843-853-2070
Fax 843-853-0044
E-mail sales@arcadiapublishing.com
For customer service and orders:
Toll-Free 1-888-313-2665

Visit us on the Internet at www.arcadiapublishing.com

Merrimack Street, Haverhill, about 1867. A lone tree fights for survival amidst the rapidly expanding and encroaching brick and granite. Most of these buildings housed shoe shops or related industries in 1867. Some still survive. Furthest left is the Essex Block (1857). To the immediate right of the tree, now shorn of its top three floors, is the Granite Block (1852) where R. H. Macy had his store. The next building became Mitchell & Co., "Haverhill's Largest Department Store," and now, minus its upper stories, it serves as the Landmark Building.

Contents

Members of the 1896 Haverhill High School Football Team. One hundred years ago, these athletes posed to show off their class sweaters with their graduation years. They live on, forever young, through the art of photography.

Introduction

Change is a given in life. It is also part of the stock in trade of an historian. Without change, life would be static, repetitive, unmemorable—boring. Thankfully, Haverhill has been a place of regular change. The many layers of its history have built up, one upon the other, each era displacing its predecessor and altering the physical appearance of the place. Though centuries old, Haverhill is not frozen in any one of its pasts: neither colonial village, mercantile town, nor industrial city. There are traces of each of these eras throughout the city, but change has been too constant to allow any more than a trace.

It is the historian's task to try to recover some of that past and bring it to life through word and print. Here the author has been especially privileged to convey a message about the past through the use of many remarkable photographs. One of the great innovations in historical methodology is the acknowledgement of the research value of the photograph. The photograph is the past forever present; it is people and places frozen in time. The camera has given us a door to the past, and the ability to re-create a time beyond individual memory. Photographs can say "this is the way it *really* was!"

This volume of historic photographs recreates the Haverhill of the second half of the nineteenth century. Some of these images date back to the 1850s and may be among the earliest camera views of the old town. Between 1850 and 1900 Haverhill grew and prospered at an astonishing rate. During this time the town had a civic life of public participation and public philanthropy that may be unequaled in its history. It welcomed newcomers—from northern New England, and from Canada and Ireland—and many of these people returned the compliment by fully immersing themselves into the city's life.

In 1996, we published a companion photographic history, *Bradford: End of an Era*. That work pondered the question of why Bradford would choose, in 1896, to be annexed to Haverhill. This book goes far to answer that question. In brief, by the end of the nineteenth century, Haverhill had much, very much, to offer those willing to join its ranks, whether they be individual newcomers or entire towns. The pictures in this book give an idea of what that included: schools, parks, hospital, library, retail stores, and workplaces.

All of these photographs are from the Special Collections of the Haverhill Public Library. They are but a small portion of the thousands of photographs contained in that incredible archive. So many and so evocative were the photos initially selected that two major decisions had to be made about the book's content. First, there would be a cut-off date of 1900; the early twentieth century would have to wait for a later volume. Second, the story of the immigrants would also be set aside for a later presentation. So, this is a photographic history of "Yankee" Haverhill—a place shaped by native New Englanders, many of them newcomers to the city. Much has changed since these pictures were taken, especially in downtown Haverhill. But, between the covers of this book, we can capture that time for a brief while, and bring it to life again.

To Greg Laing, Howard Curtis and all their predecessors
who have made the Haverhill Public Library's Special Collections
a research treasure trove, but especially to Greg and Howard.
We are immeasurably indebted to them.
And to the trustees of the Haverhill Public Library
for their cooperation and encouragement
in allowing me to present the library's treasures to the public.

One

The Old Downtown

The Heart of Old Haverhill. Main Street about the year 1857. This may be one of the earliest views of the old town. The majority of the clapboard buildings are in an early nineteenth-century style. The tower in the left center is on the town hall, which was built in 1848. Behind the V-shaped Common is the old First Parish Church. Downtown Haverhill must have looked like this for much of the first half of the nineteenth century.

Elm (or White's) Corner, 1867. Ten years after the previous photo, brick and stone have begun to dominate the architecture of this commercial area. The large building in the right center is the Eagle House. The steeple behind it is on the Centre Congregational Church. The women in the foreground stand near the bridge to Bradford. The bridge was covered, and a toll was charged for its use.

The Elm Corner Drug Store. Edward G. Frothingham (1837–1931), the owner, was a Civil War veteran, state legislator, governor's councilor, and involved in almost every civic and fraternal group in Haverhill. He epitomized the kind of involved local businessmen that characterized Haverhill in the second half of the nineteenth century.

"Colonel" William H. Brown. From 1819 to 1872 Brown was innkeeper of the Eagle House, Haverhill's most distinguished hotel. Brown was widely known for his hospitality and for the fish dinners on his menu. He made a point to serve the first salmon caught each summer in the Merrimack River.

The Eagle House Hotel on Main Street. This establishment was built in 1800 for merchant James Duncan Jr., and it was considered Haverhill's grandest house in its time. The ground floor and seventy-five additional rooms were added after 1819 when it became a hotel. The magnificent carved eagle in the gable peak is now at the Haverhill Historical Society. Furnishings from two of the Duncan-era rooms are in the Metropolitan Museum in New York City.

The Residence of Reverend George W. Kelly, 49 Main Street. This elegant Italianate style brick house was built about 1857. Reverend Kelly, a retired Congregational minister, lived in the right half of the house. In later years, the building served as the Haverhill District Court. It was razed in 1967 as part of urban renewal.

A Familiar Sight in Old Haverhill. Reverend George W. Kelly and his Saint Bernard dog take their evening stroll on Main Street. The Federal-era house to Kelly's left was that of Dr. Kendall Flint, a local physician.

The Front Vestibule of the James Henry Duncan House. This home stood at the corner of Main and Summer Streets, where the public library now stands. The photograph shows the interior of the house as it was in the early 1890s when it became the Pentucket Club.

The Duncan House. This dwelling was originally designed for Moses Moody by architect John Haviland of Philadelphia. The front part of it is done in the Greek Revival style, for which Haviland was renowned. The ionic columns, Palladian window, and handsome double staircase reflected the highest style of the first quarter of the nineteenth century.

The Shaw-Nichols House. This house was located at the opposite corner of Main and Summer Streets from the Duncan(Pentucket Club) House. In the eighteenth century, when this was the parsonage for the Reverend John Shaw, his nephew and future president John Quincy Adams lived here and was tutored by his uncle. The pediment and columns shown in this photograph were a later addition to the facade. The structure was taken down in the early twentieth century to be replaced by a new high school, now the city hall.

The Newcombs at Home. Mr. and Mrs. John Newcomb lived in a three-story Federal double house next to the Shaw-Nichols House on Summer Street. When the new high school was to be constructed, one-half of the house was destroyed, but the then-widow Newcomb saved her half and had it moved around the corner to Newcomb Street where it still stands. The wallpaper shown in the photograph was from Paris, and is now in the Museum of Fine Arts, Boston. The carved sofa is at the Buttonwoods Museum.

The Haverhill Common about 1867. Baseball is already a popular game. This view is from the north, or Crescent Place, side. The Common was bought by the town in 1837 from the First Parish. The wooden fence and the elm trees seen here date from 1848. In the rear are the new Town Hall (1861) and the Wesleyan Methodist Church (1854).

The Common from Another Perspective. Looking north, the camera has included the First Parish Church in its original position, and, to the left, the home of the missionary pioneer Harriet Atwood Newell. The Shaw-Nichols House is just visible on the right. But the center of attention in this, and the previous picture, are the young boys at play.

Haverhill's First High School. Opened in 1827 to accommodate the private Haverhill Academy, it was acquired by the School District #1 for a free, public high school in 1844. It was opened to the entire town in 1855. When this photo was taken, a new high school, built in 1872, stood on nearby Crescent Place and the old Academy had become the Whittier Grammar School, in honor of the old school's most distinguished alumnus.

Haverhill High School, Class of 1868. The small number of graduates reflects an era when high school was a privilege of the few. The males would probably go on to college or professional school. The females might spend a year at a "finishing" school, such as the nearby Bradford Academy. The severe hair styles and clothing makes this group of seventeen-and eighteen-year olds look far older than their chronological age.

16

The Hat Factory of Eben Mitchell. In mid-nineteenth-century Haverhill, hats competed with shoes as principal product. Mitchell (1818–1896) located his company behind the Town Hall and employed many of the new Irish immigrants. High school was not an option for these young people.

Merrimack Street in the Old Downtown, about 1857. Merrimack Street was a residential area well into the mid-1800s. The first brick buildings went up on the river side, principally for the growing shoe-making business. Others quickly followed. The trees in the background mark the dividing line between the industrial and residential street.

Transition! By the 1867 date of this photograph, the trees were gone from the south (or river) side of Merrimack Street. In their place was this handsome row of uniform, harmonious shoe factories with the granite cornices of the Greek Revival style. The trees on the right mark the Saltonstall property.

The 1788 Saltonstall House. Dr. Nathaniel Saltonstall, of Haverhill's pre-eminent colonial family, built this home which graced Merrimack Street with its Georgian elegance and sweeping lawns for almost one hundred years. In 1871 it was moved to the shores of Lake Saltonstall, shown above, as the family surrendered to encroaching industrialism around their old location.

Cellar Hole Of The Saltonstall House. All that remained of the Saltonstall Mansion in December 1871 was this spot being viewed by passersby to the left. And, with the house, went the last of the trees on Merrimack Street. The old town was changing.

First Baptist Church on Merrimack Street, about 1865. This was the third building built by the Baptist Society. It was in a Gothic Revival style with pointed arches. The towering steeple was a landmark for miles around. The church was located at the corner of hilly Pecker Street and the builders have taken advantage of the grade to elevate the entire structure well above street level, thus permitting the flights of steps to the entrance.

A Fraternal Organization Parades to the Baptist Church, about 1876. There are some wooden houses still evident but just east of the houses is the three-story brick structure, next to the front gabled building, which replaced the Saltonstall Mansion.

The City Hotel, about 1875. A touch of elegance in the old downtown, this new hotel supplanted the Eagle House, just as Merrimack Street supplanted Main Street as the center of town. This was a delightful Italianate building with cast-iron pillars on the first floor, and a wonderful balcony from which to view the passing parade of hansom cabs. How Street and the Masonic Temple are to the right, and the steeple of the First Baptist Church is visible.

The Washington Square End of Merrimack Street. This photo was taken about 1855 when Little River still flowed freely through Washington Square. All of these buildings date from the late eighteenth, or early nineteenth, century. The house on the right was replaced by the still-extant, four-story, brick Franklin Block in 1857.

William H. Butler House. Mr. Butler, a "Decorative House Painter And Paper Hanger," occupied this house in the 1880s. It was originally built by David Marsh in the late eighteenth century and was located at 171 Merrimack Street, on the north side, close to Washington Square.

The Annual Spring Flood of The Little River. This yearly occurrence was controlled in 1855 by covering the mouth of the river to create Washington Square and directing the flow through a stone arch into the Merrimack River. The arch (above) was built in 1877 and extended the cover to the banks of the Merrimack creating Washington Square Park.

Washington Square, September 1867. The Odd Fellows, a fraternal organization, gather by the Liberty Pole at the South Christian Church. The pole was made from a ship's mast and stood in the square from 1851 to 1872. The South Christian Church (in the back) supplemented its Sunday collection by leasing out the ground floor to a butcher shop. Washington Street (on the left) was still residential in 1867.

The Haverhill Police, 1870. The old town offered few municipal services. Though the town had reached the 10,000 population mark as early as 1860, it had only a handful of men to keep law and order. They are, from left to right, as follows: (front) Lewis Holt, Marshall George Geary, and Edward Fowler; (back) Ira Carter, Phineas Davis, Captain John Collins, and Daniel Smith.

Private Militia Groups. This kind of organization was very popular in the 1850s. It was an excuse to wear a uniform and march around, accompanied by a fife and drum corps such as this one, on a weekly basis. Neither the group, nor the musicians, have yet been identified.

Two

More of the Old Town

Old and New Haverhill. Beyond the Main Street/Merrimack Street center of mid-nineteenth century Haverhill there remained much physical evidence of the older mercantile and farming community. Yet traces of a newer Haverhill were already in evidence. This is a view to the east side of Main Street, which was the earliest settled area in town. The two brick houses (right, center) in this 1867 photograph remain on Stage Street to the present day. The District Court now stands where the jumble of houses and sheds are (foreground). Beyond this congested area are the "new" (in 1867) houses on Summer Street, with their spacious lawns and panoramic views over the river valley.

A Remnant of the Past. This is the Golden Ball Tavern on Water Street. It was originally the mansion house of merchant John White and was the center of society in Revolutionary-era Haverhill. The house was once surrounded by gardens as far as the river's edge.

Moore Street, off of Water Street. This was a working class area of simple houses. Above, a young child peers through the screen door, two more stand beyond their father at the gate, and four curious neighborhood children watch the photographer at work.

Beach's Soap Factory, at the Corner of Mill and Water Streets. The photograph dates from the 1880s. Lurandus Beach, president of the factory, lived on Lawrence Street, near Round Pond.

The White-Clement House, at 86 Mill Street. This was the family seat of one of Haverhill's founding families. James Davis White (in tall hat and sash) is about to participate in the 1867 Odd Fellows Parade (see p. 23). This fine old Georgian house remains on the same location but has been moved back from the street.

Doctor Irah E. Chase (1831–1919) came to Haverhill in 1853 after completing his medical studies. He traveled extensively throughout Europe and the Near East during his life. The curios collected in his travels were willed to the Public Library and are the basis of the children's museum collection.

Doctor Chase's House, at 107 Winter Street. Built soon after his arrival in Haverhill, this house was designed in an Italianate style. Winter Street was one of the best addresses in town in the mid-nineteenth century.

Renovations. The Second Empire-style mansard roof became very popular in the 1860s. Dr. Irah Chase renovated his Winter Street house with the new style roof, which had been introduced in Paris and widely imitated. The style effectively added a third story to the building. Dr. Chase later moved to Park Street and gave this house to the YWCA.

Post-Civil-War Haverhill. The Civil War was a defining event in the transition from the old town to the new city of Haverhill. Beyond the cost of human lives, the war also had strong economic and social effects. Those who served came home to a newly-emerging and thriving shoe industry. And through such veterans' organizations as the Grand Army of the Republic, the former soldiers renewed a concept of community and civic commitment. This is James How of Post 47 in his G.A.R. uniform.

The Soldiers Monument, Monument Square. This was the first public sculpture ever erected in town. It was dedicated in 1869, about one year before this photograph was taken. The view is from Pond Street, later renamed Kenoza Avenue, and the house shown in the rear is located on Main Street.

The North Parish Congregational Church Choir. Beyond the downtown, Haverhill was divided into the North, East, and West Parishes. These areas were rural and agrarian, and communities were centered around their parish churches. This picture, taken from a stereopticon, shows the choir in 1880 preparing for the 150th anniversary of the parish.

Hauling Stone, North Parish. Downtown Haverhill was a place of steam engines and gas lights, but life in the parishes followed many of the old ways. The Brickett Farm, 1115 Main Street, is in the background of this photograph. Though the image is dated c. 1900, neither the house nor the men's technique for removing the boulder appear to have been altered from the style of the previous half-century.

The Griffin House at 224 Groveland Street. Access to the East Parish was along Kenoza Avenue/Amesbury Road, or Groveland Street/East Broadway. The gradual suburbanization of Groveland Street is seen in this delightful Second Empire house. Its style—with asymmetrical form, mansard roof, and tower—is in marked contrast to the eighteenth-century farmhouses and Greek Revival cottages that were its neighbors.

Rocks Village Looking East to West Newbury. Rocks Village was the most north-easterly part of Haverhill. Separated from the downtown by farms and gravel-filled hills, and with no immediate access to the railroad, it developed at a slower pace than the downtown. Without industry, it maintained an eighteenth-century village lifestyle well into the twentieth century. The covered bridge, seen here, lasted until 1913.

Volunteer Firemen, Rocks Village, 1898. The communal values of village life continued in Rocks Village, decades after downtown Haverhill had developed extensive municipal services. The thirty-two men who posed with the Protector No. 3 Hand Engine probably constituted most of the able-bodied males of the village.

The Thomas West House, 229 Kenoza Avenue. This Federal house on the farm near Kenoza Lake was one of several properties that West owned, including the Golden Ball Tavern (see p. 26).

The West House Transformed. When the Shaw-Nichols House (see p. 14) was razed in 1908 to make way for a new high school, the pediment and columns were removed by Edward Brickett and added to the West House, which Brickett had purchased. Thus, a part of historic old Haverhill continues to grace the landscape.

Winnekenni Castle. Dr. James R. Nichols (1819–1888) graduated from Dartmouth and spent his career as a researcher and successful inventor. In 1863, he purchased an estate on Kenoza Lake which he turned into an experimental farm. Then, with granite found on the estate, he built this medieval style "castle" on the highest part of the land to serve as his summer home.

Dr. James R. Nichols and His Daughter, Mrs. Harriet Cupples, at the Cascades. The Cascades was part of the ornamental park designed to enhance the landscape at Winnekenni Castle.

The Kenoza Lake Club's Annual Picnic, about 1868. Great Pond, or Kenoza Lake, is one of Haverhill's natural treasures. The club, founded in 1807, was an association of those who enjoyed fishing. The "Old Stone House" (rear) was built in 1859 on the eastern shore of the lake. Each year the town's businessmen and their families gathered here for a feast of fish chowder. The club re-christened the lake from Great Pond to "Kenoza," which means "lake of the pickerel."

Three

Transformation!

Before the Change. In 1850, Haverhill was a small town. By 1900, it was a flourishing city, nationally known for its shoe industry. Most of that transformation occurred in the two decades from 1870 to 1890. The town became a city, municipal institutions and services flourished, and the physical appearance of the downtown was dramatically altered. This photograph, taken before 1867, provides a last look at the old town. It was taken where Washington Street and River Street meet. The nearer bridge was the 1839 railroad bridge. The train tracks ran at street level to the original 1838 station which is immediately in front of the long white building. At this date, Washington Street was still a mix of domestic and industrial buildings.

The 1867 Boston and Maine Railroad Station. This station was designed by noted local architect Josiah Littlefield. The station would be the center from which the changes would radiate in Haverhill. The railroad provided an essential link to the outside. Raw materials arrived and finished goods were shipped. Ambitious Yankees from northern New England, and immigrants freshly arrived to the port of Boston, made their way via the rails to Haverhill and, they hoped, to success and security.

Edwin Bowley (1822–1884). A grocer and investor in real estate, Bowley was convinced that the presence of the railroad station meant that the "Mount" Washington area would become the most prestigious address in town.

Bowley's Mount Washington Park, about 1870. This block of brick row houses with the new-style mansard roof, at the top of Washington Avenue, was meant to suggest Boston's Beacon Hill and its Louisburgh Square. Bowley's plans called for similar town houses on each side of the park.

Alas, for Edwin Bowley! Haverhill's moneyed families chose instead to build their new homes in the Summer Street area, thus creating the "Highlands." Bowley might have found some consolation in the new grammar school on Washington Street named for him. (Bailey photograph, 1890.)

The South Christian Church in Washington Square. The church stood at the junction of Washington and Essex streets and was surrounded by numerous wood frame houses. The most dramatic change in Haverhill would take place in this area.

Ayer Hat Factory, about 1866. Some industry had begun to filter into the area by the train station, but many of the buildings were of wood construction. The muddy street is a reminder of how little public tax money was spent on the area. This building was torn down in 1873.

Moses How (1819–1896), Shoe Industry Pioneer. Shoemaking in Haverhill had been a domestic industry with individual shoemakers working their craft in "ten-footers"—wooden shops behind their houses. Moses How, who had been in the coal and lumber business, took up shoe manufacturing in 1853 on Merrimack Street. He introduced the factory system of production, the Singer Sewing Machine, and the McKay sole stitching machine, thus turning shoe-making from a handicraft to an industry.

Caleb Duston Hunking (1805–1872), for whom the Bradford Middle School and the high school scholarships are named, was another pioneer in the early shoe industry. He also had the foresight to help finance R. H. Macy when that founder of the landmark department store made the move from the building he shared with Hunking on Merrimack Street to New York City and into the history books.

Civil-War-Era Shoe Industry Building on Washington Street. A few buildings in brick with granite trim and cast iron pillars had been built such as this one, owned by Albert L. Kimball of Bradford. The running row of rounded arches was typical of many of these new buildings. Kimball stands in the center of the back row surrounded by cutters and a stitcher from his shop.

Wilton H. Carleton. A leather sole manufacturer, Mr. Carleton is shown at ease in the office of his new factory at 58 Washington Street. His casual pose and air of success suggest the potential prosperity of the new shoe city.

Disaster! Overnight, Haverhill's success and bright future went up in flames. A horrific fire wiped out all the buildings on Washington Street from Washington Square to Railroad Square. One life was lost along with over a million and a half dollars worth of property. Three thousand workers were without jobs. This was the scene on February 18, 1882, the morning after the fire, as viewed from Washington Square.

Clearing the Debris. Within days of the great conflagration, the rubble was being cleared. Every manufacturer was back in business using whatever makeshift arrangement could be found and rebuilding plans were under way. This is the view from partway down Washington Street looking east. The greater part of the ruins have already been removed.

Three Survivors of the 1882 Fire. The inferno also destroyed one side of Wingate Street that abutted Washington Street but spared these three buildings. The Gardner Block faces onto Railroad Square. The other two buildings are on Wingate Street. All three remain standing to the present.

44

Surviving Building. The Currier-Sanders Block at Railroad Square was the only building on Washington Street to survive the great fire. It had been built only five years earlier (1877) from a design by Josiah Littlefield. The running arches, the brick pilasters that rise vertically through the three floors, and the decorative brick work across the top reflect the architecture of Renaissance Italy.

Recovery! The Pilling Block on Wingate Street was the first to be completed after the fire. The top floor was the making room. The third floor was the cutting room. The right side of the second floor was the stitching room, dominated by women, and the left half was the finishing room. The first floor, right side, was the sole leather department. The left side was the office.

The gentleman with the hat between the middle doors is John Pilling, the owner. To his right, holding an account book in her hand, is fifteen-year-old bookkeeper Grace Horne, who donated this photograph to the public library.

Washington Square, after the Fire. A five-story hotel, the Webster (later re-named the Whittier) crowns the newly rebuilt square. Symbolically, a horse-drawn fire engine was passing as the photographer took this picture.

Shoe City, Haverhill. Washington Street was completely re-built within a year. This reveals much about the optimistic mood of the shoemen, and the support of financial and government leaders. The majority of the plans were by two local architects, Josiah Littlefield and C. Willis Damon. All the buildings are in a uniform Queen Anne, or Victorian, style with decorative brick work. The above photograph was taken in July 1890 when Haverhill celebrated its 250th anniversary.

Close Up of Decorative Queen Anne style Brickwork. This is the Goodrich and Porter building at 70 Washington Street. The fancy brick work is a tribute not only to its designers, but also to the many talented Italian brick masons who were imported from New York and other areas to provide the skill needed.

The Taylor-Prescott Block, 108–114 Washington Street. This block was built as an almost-replica of its next neighbor, the Currier-Sanders Block (see p. 45), which had survived the fire. The thriving shoe industry drew many related businesses to the downtown, none more important than the United Shoe Machinery Co. which held a monopoly on the stitching machines and would only lease, not sell, each one.

The Savignac Brick Yard, Rosemont Street. Haverhill had a long history of making bricks from local clay. The ready availability of these locally-made bricks facilitated the rapid recovery of "Shoe City" and also guaranteed the aesthetically pleasing facades of warm red brick.

Charles Savignac (1840-1906). An immigrant from Quebec in 1859, Mr. Savignac did as many of his compatriots did, going to work in the brickyards that were throughout the North Parish and in Plaistow, NH. In a brief time, he had his own works and soon became one of the largest manufacturers of bricks in the north east. Savignac is the gentleman in the bowler hat with his thumbs hooked into his vest, standing at right center.

50

Haverhill Shoeworkers: An Eclectic Mix. Irish and French-Canadians had been in town since the mid-nineteenth century. African-Americans came after the Civil War. Italians, Greeks, and Armenians arrived in the 1890s. The burgeoning shoe shops welcomed them all. The man on the far left is Edward "Sport" Harden. His brother-in-law, Varris Sanville, is also in the picture, as is Sanville's young son. The shop is probably that of Field, Thayer, and Maguire, located at the rear of 132 Washington Street.

A Cutting Room, 1900. The shoe cutters held the best paying and most desirable jobs in a shoe shop, as the white shirts and neckties demonstrate.

The Winchell Shoe Factory, Locust Street, 1895. Success brought change. The shops on Washington Street became too small and too limiting. Businessmen began to move out of the downtown along Essex Street and further west to River Street Some even moved out of town. James Winchell began in the shoe business in 1858 when he was nineteen, with factories on Merrimack Street, and pre- and post-fire Washington Street. In 1891 he opened this building on Locust Street. It was the largest in the city, with 84,000 square feet of floor space occupied by a single firm.

Linwood Cemetery.
James H. Winchell (inset) did not have long to enjoy his new factory. Almost five years to the day of its opening, he died suddenly while attending the theatre in Boston. The photograph offers us a rare look at burial practices of one hundred years ago. There is some irony to the floral tributes from his employees, for Winchell was one of the main targets of the city's most famous shoe strike in 1895.

The Business Side of the Shoe Industry. Howard Clark (seated) was James H. Winchell's junior partner. His home was at 44 Arlington Street. The man behind him is Tom Jewell, shipping clerk, who lived at 45 White Street. Both are wearing long "dusters" over their formal business clothes.

Women Shoe Stitchers at A. L. Wiswell and Co.'s Stitching Room. A stitcher of shoes had a status not equaled by her sisters in the textile factories near Haverhill. For one thing, the work could be done while seated. Also, because little capital outlay was required to rent floor space and lease stitching machines, many stitching rooms were owned and operated by women. Stitchers had such a respected position in the town that, in 1894/95, when stitchers at some of the biggest shops in town (Chick Bros., Spaulding's, and Winchell's) went on a long, drawn-out strike, the sympathy of the community was with the women, not the manufacturers.

Chick Brothers Shoe Factory. This establishment was built at the furthest developed edge of River Street, next to the circus grounds. This was to be the limit of the downtown factory system and the land between Chick's and Railroad Square became congested with multi-family tenement houses for the workers in the factory. Though trolley lines criss-crossed the city by 1890, the average shoe worker could not afford the fare on a daily basis, and had to live within walking distance of his shop.

Lamont and Nellie Chick in India. Chick, like Winchell, Wiswell, Hunking, How, and most of the city's "shoe men," was an outsider who migrated to Haverhill from small-town New England. So successful was he that he maintained a winter home in Miami, a summer home in Maine, and regularly traveled to Europe and the Orient.

J. P. Stevens' Pentucket Mill. Haverhill wasn't only a shoe town. Though it would never rival Lawrence, Lowell, or Manchester, it did have a share of the textile industry. Ezekiel Hale had a textile mill in operation by the Little River as early as 1804. Nathaniel Stevens acquired this 1835 building in 1855. The Stevens family continued to operate the mill until the middle of the twentieth century. Shown above is the spinning room.

The Weaving Room at Stevens Pentucket Mill. Rows of silent looms await the weavers. This 1895 photograph shows something else— the building is lit by electricity and each loom has its own lamp.

Four

Grand and Glorious Architecture

Optimism and Innovation. The trends which transformed Haverhill's economy in the late nineteenth century extended into its architecture. A new style came into vogue that was as flamboyant and expansive as the city's mood. Collectively it is known as Victorian, or Queen Anne. It revelled in decorative surfaces, asymmetrical shapes, dormers, towers, stained glass, and the thousands of new designs that millwork could now offer to builders. Above is the Rufus Chase House on Main Street designed by C. Willis Damon. It is a rare example of the variation known as the Stick Style. The house is now the Dole, Childs, and Shaw Funeral Home.

Removal of the First Baptist Church. Out with the old, in with the new. By 1883, the church building was out of style and in the wrong location. The congregation agreed to move to a new location, closer to the stylish Highlands area, and the Merrimack Street church was razed.

The Academy of Music Building. This building replaced the Baptist Church. Music and theater filled the auditorium and small shops filled the rest of the space. Above is a sketch of Haverhill's new entertainment center from an 1890s advertising booklet. The building on the left is the Masonic Temple at the corner of How Street.

The New First Baptist Church, Main Street. The design is in the Romanesque style popularized by famed Boston architect Henry Hobson Richardson. It is reminiscent of the early twelfth-century style of French cathedrals that preceded the Gothic style.

Number 69 Summer Street. Romanesque architecture was not as popular for houses, but this one (shown in 1976), built for hotel owner Richard Webster, demonstrates its possibilities. The building now houses the local American Red Cross chapter.

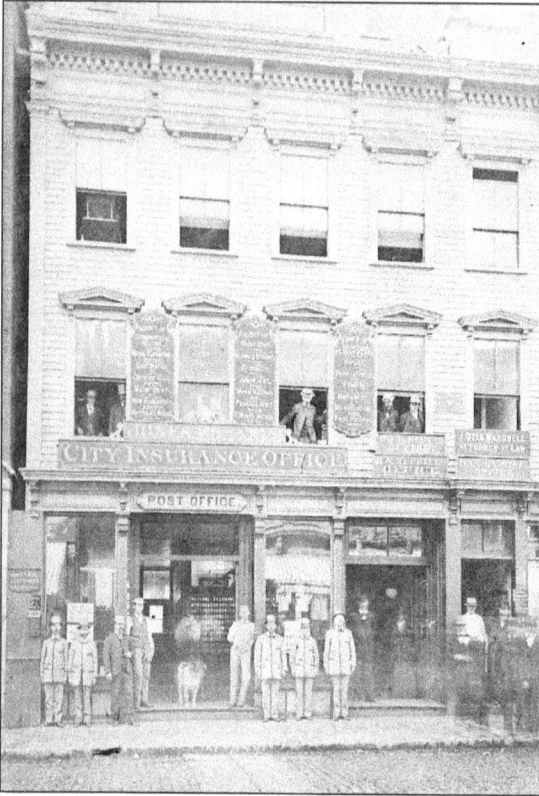

The Old Post Office at 60 Merrimack Street, about 1885. The postal service shared space with lawyers and insurance offices.

The New Post Office in Washington Square, Built in the 1890s in the Romanesque Style. McKee's lunch wagon, the forerunner of the diner or fast food restaurant, is the white vehicle to the right. The Franklin Block can be seen on the left.

The Daggett Building. This was one of the finest pieces of commercial architecture in Haverhill, built in 1888. The fifty-six-room building, designed by C. Willis Damon, was the city's first office building. It contained all the latest features, including the city's first passenger elevator, electric lights, speaking tubes, and call buttons. The exterior was composed of pressed brick laid in red mortar and trimmed with brownstone and terra-cotta panels. It was razed during Urban Renewal.

The James E. Gale House, at the Corner of Summer Street and Highland Avenue. A classic Queen Anne house, it disregards symmetry in shape but still achieves a wonderful balance. With its rounded arches and Moorish arches, bay windows, porches, and colored glass, it is a joyful house to view and a magnificent example of its style. The building is now the H. L. Farmer Funeral Home. (Nichols photograph.)

The Austin P. Nichols House, 4 Highland Avenue with its delightful half-tower on the second floor. Nichols, the son of Dr. James Nichols, was publisher of the Boston Journal of Chemistry. He was also an excellent photographer. Many of the photographs in this book are from his collection.

The Samuel Hosford House, 48 Park Street. This home is built in the Shingle Style, another variant of Queen Anne, which was becoming popular at seaside resorts such as Newport, RI. Austin Nichols took this photograph in 1889. The building no longer exists.

The Grandest of the Grand. This is the Queen Anne-style Gardner House at One Windsor Street. The area had once been open pasture and the lack of trees of any size magnifies the appearance of the great house built in 1887. (Nichols photograph, 1891.)

Close Up of the Tower. Decorative shingles and other design touches have made the house at One Windsor Street a prize. S. Porter Gardner, who built the Gardner Block in Railroad Square, was the first owner of the house. Later, shoeman C. H. Hayes acquired it and added the weather vane with the letter "H." (Photograph taken in 1976.)

Goodrich-McNamara House, at 3 Windsor Street. Just as the Shingle Style was meant to evoke the "simple cottages" of Newport millionaires, so this style, with its rustic field stones, was meant to remind its viewers of the "lodges" that other millionaires built in the Adirondack mountains.

C. W. Arnold House, 25 Westland Terrace. Interest in the more flamboyant Victorian styles faded at the end of the century. It was replaced by a revival of Georgian and Federal styles in what was popularly called Colonial Revival. It is almost redundant to note that Charles W. Arnold was a shoe manufacturer who came to Haverhill from northern New England. The house was taken down in 1973.

Winter Panorama. Mill Street, Kenoza Avenue, and Lake Saltonstall (aka Plug Pond) are shown about 1900. The houses shown range the age spectrum from the 1712 Ayer House (left center) to the 1895 Arnold House (uppermost right). In the center, closest to the lake, is the Shingle

Style house that architect C. Willis Damon designed for himself. Before the advent of the "auto age," streets were not plowed, but rolled, or "pounded down" to allow horse-drawn pungs or sleighs rapid passage.

New Designs and New Architecture Were Not Limited to the downtown and the Highlands. They could be found in Bradford, on Mount Washington, and, as here, the Upper Main Street area. Shown above is the meticulously landscaped garden of William Morton at 10 Columbia Park. Morton, shown seated on his porch, was a fresco painter and interior decorator with a flair for landscape design. Columbia Park was built with a central mall running its length in the style of Boston's Commonwealth Avenue.

Jackson Webster House, 39 North Avenue. Large elegant houses continued to be built throughout the 1890s as Highlandville on Upper Main Street, and then the Walnut Square area became accessible, thanks to the trolley. The Webster House has much of the Colonial Revival about it, but the tower, with its "eyes," is pure Queen Anne flamboyance. Webster worked for B. F. Leighton & Co., wholesale grocers.

Five

A Thriving
Retail Economy

"Let's Go to the People's Wedding. Everybody Will Be There." And, indeed, it looks as though they were. On April 7, 1892, the People's Furniture Co. at White's Corner staged a public relations extravaganza. It sponsored a public wedding of a young local couple and invited the whole city to attend. On the raised platform, under the wedding bell, the couple exchanged their vows before the mayor and a sizeable part of the local population. The furniture store received days of publicity from the event, the couple received gifts from the store, and the entire downtown must have benefitted from the presence of so many. Nothing has changed so much in Haverhill as the downtown. In this chapter we will take a walk from White's Corner to Railroad Square and view a commercial life that is irrevocably gone.

J. O. Batchelder's Express Wagon. The wagon is shown in front of the Chase Block at 19–25 Merrimack Street. Note the juxtaposition, under the awning, of the signs for candies and for a dentist! (Bailey photograph.)

From the Chase Block to White's Corner, c. 1895. The People's Furniture Co. is the light-colored building on the right. In the distance, on Water Street, is the old Golden Ball Tavern. (Bailey photograph.)

Thomas Bailey's Drug Store,
23 Merrimack Street, formerly
Geo. A. Kimball & Co. On the left
is a soda fountain and a counter full
of cigars. On the right are beauty
and photographic supplies. In other
words, this was a typical modern
drug store. (Bailey photograph.)

Thomas H. Bailey (1851–1922). Mr.
Bailey came to Haverhill as a child. He
operated a drug store on Merrimack
Street for many years, but he gave as
much time to his hobby of photography.
Many of his photographs are in the
library's Special Collections and are used
liberally throughout this book.

The J. W. And D. R. Bennett
Shoe Store. Located at
18 Merrimack Street, this
shoe store was a fixture for
decades in the downtown.
Jeremiah Bennett lived at
46 Groveland Street. Thomas
Burnham (see p. 102) became a
partner of the Bennetts in 1871.

Bela H. Jacobs at His Dry Goods
Store, 40 Merrimack Street,
about 1885. By 1889, he was
in the investments business at
103 Merrimack Street. Jacobs lived
at 72 White Street. He later moved
to 141 Main Street.

Wilson & Tuck's Boston Branch Grocery Store was at the corner of Fleet Street. This picture is from an 1878 stereopticon, which might explain why the "best Vermont butter" was only 19¢ a pound.

Parade on Merrimack Street About 1885. The plumed hats on the band and marchers suggest a fraternal group such as the Knights of Pythias or the Hibernians. The building with the gable to the street is at the corner of Fleet Street which was the first street on the north side of Merrimack Street until removed by Urban Renewal. The line across the photograph is caused by a crack in the glass plate negative from which this was copied.

N. Woodburn Nichols and Bainbridge Morse at the Nichols and Morse Clothing Store, 56–62 Merrimack Street. Nichols lived at 3 Kenoza Avenue, and Morse resided at 55 Mt. Vernon Street.

Rowe & Emerson Clothing Co., 68 Merrimack Street. Standing in the doorway are Bert LeFavor, Percy Morgan, Emma Sawyer, and Harry Johnson. Owner Henry Rowe had a home at 265 Main Street and his partner, Hervey Emerson, lived at 57 Webster Street.

C. C. Morse & Son, 67 Merrimack
Street. Books, works of art, picture
frames, newspapers—Morse had
them all. The store had gas lighting
fixtures, and, on the floor, we can
see the vent for a hot air furnace.

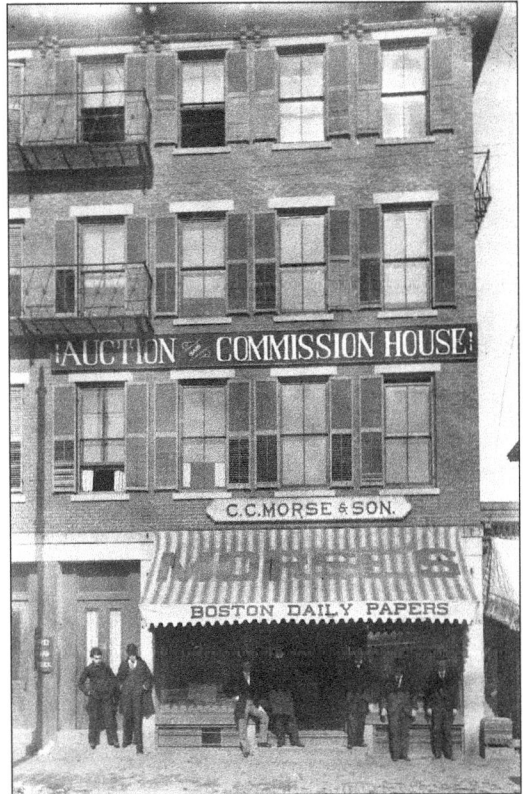

Exterior of the C. C. Morse & Son Shop.
By the time this picture was taken, the
downtown had brick sidewalks and the
street was covered with paving stones.
George Morse, the proprietor, lived at
18 Webster Street.

James C. Bates, Jeweler, 79 Merrimack Street, about 1892. Bates was one of more than a dozen jewelers in Haverhill in the 1890s. His home was at 69 Auburn Street.

Pond & Hamilton, Crockery and Kitchen Furnishings. The contents of the store appear to have included sleds, doll carriages, and rocking horses. The store was at 74 Merrimack Street. The photograph, which dates from *c.* 1895, was taken by Herbert Ramsell, whose regular occupation was as a trolley car driver.

Jessie Fullers' Store, Kid Gloves and Fancy Work, 79 Merrimack Street, about 1895. As is evident from this photograph, Haverhill's downtown had a small shop for everything and anything. Mr. Fuller lived at 51 Vestry Street

Western Union Telegraph and W. S. Willey & Co. Sewing Machines at 198–200 Merrimack Street (the river side). A wonderful mix in this photograph: the policeman in his old-style helmet, the men in their summer straw "boaters," the telegram delivery boys in their knickers and caps, and the women clerks—a reminder that females were now a part of the retail scene.

Lincoln Hall at 153–155 Merrimack Street. The building is decorated for the 250th anniversary celebration in 1890. Lyons and Sawyer, the shop in the left corner, sports an authentic carved Indian, so it must be a cigar store.

Looking West from the Daggett Building. Austin Nichols captured this view of Merrimack Street as it stretches into Washington Street on a winter's day. The buildings on the left have undergone a few alterations but still have much of their harmonious uniformity which made them so pleasing to the eye. (see p. 18.)

W. McKee's Lunch Wagon. After walking and window shopping the length of Merrimack Street, the weary shopper could be refreshed with a cup of tea and a roll at McKee's lunch before boarding a trolley car for the ride home.

Gerson & Feinberg, Home Furnishings, 103 Washington Street As shoe manufacturers like James Winchell moved out to larger quarters, a greater diversification of businesses sprouted on Washington Street. Charles M. Gerson stands in front of his furniture store in the Tilton Block in the early years of this family business that would become a Haverhill institution.

Hickey's Shoe and Leather Exchange Restaurant, across from Gerson's Furniture Co., at 106 Washington Street. If the interior strikes a familiar chord, it should, for more recently this has been The Tap, and the Riverside House of Brews.

Professor Bill, Artist Bootblack, 116 Washington Street. William Mobley (1873–1948, second right), came to Haverhill from Kentucky in 1894 and began his business in the shadow of the train station. The business flourished, he invested wisely in real estate and the Stutz Motor Co., and he was a confidante and advisor to local politicians and businessmen.

The Life Saving Station Cafe on the Wingate Street Side of Railroad Square. This establishment was a welcome sight to arriving train passengers. "Our specialities, Steaks and Chops, Lobsters and Oysters, Meals Served Any Time."

The Railroad Square Building. This building contained a series of small shops including the Life Saving Station Cafe. This area is now a small park. The building to the left is the Bragg Block. In the rear of the photograph can be seen parts of the Taylor-Prescott and Currier-Sanders Blocks.

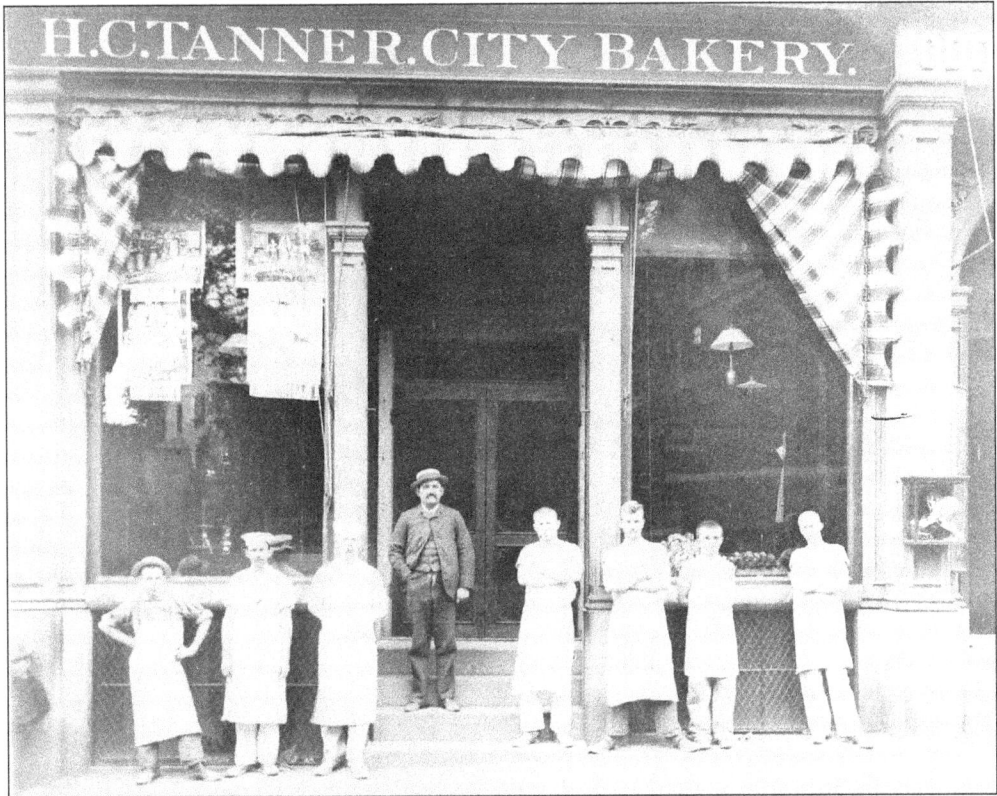

Back to Main Street, and Haverhill's Best-Known Caterer. The H. C. Tanner Bakery was next to the Odd Fellows Hall at 24 Main Street. Henry Tanner (1843–1911) had learned his trade in Cork, Ireland. He came to Haverhill in 1877 and quickly established his reputation for fine food. Tanner is shown here in suit and hat standing with his bakers.

H. C. Tanner Tent and Dinner. The tent stands in readiness for the great banquet that culminated Haverhill's 250th anniversary of its settlement in 1640. The entire anniversary celebration was a brilliant display of the great community spirit and civic enthusiasm in the transformed Haverhill of the late nineteenth century.

James H. Cummings Furnishing Undertaker, across the street from Tanner's Bakery at 37 Main Street. Funerals had become public rather than private family affairs in the post-Civil War era, and a number of undertakers competed for business. The hack that would carry the coffin had to be dignified but noticeable. The horses drawing the hack would be decked out in plumes and the hack driver would be somberly attired with black crepe wrapped around his tall hat. Mr. Cummings, the bearded man in the center, softens the somber tone of his profession, with his doffed hat and smile.

Six

Private Funding, Public Institutions

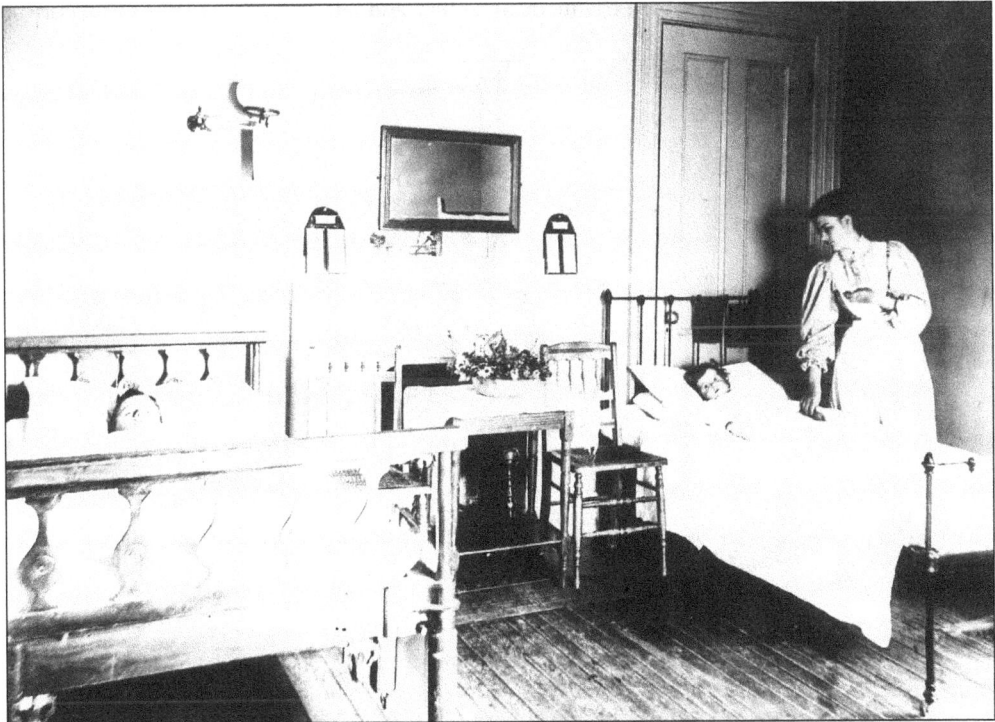

Community Involvement in Every Aspect of Life. The hallmark of Haverhill in the second half of the nineteenth century was community involvement. Private citizens took the lead in establishing a wide range of new institutions for the benefit of the public. This is the Children's Ward of the Haverhill City Hospital which opened in 1887. (George photograph.)

Haverhill's New Hospital. The Former Franklin Brickett House (or Midlake Farm), was situated between Round Pond and Kenoza Lake. The hospital was renamed in 1898 in honor of E. J. M. Hale who first proposed the medical facility and left money and land to support it. (Bailey photograph.)

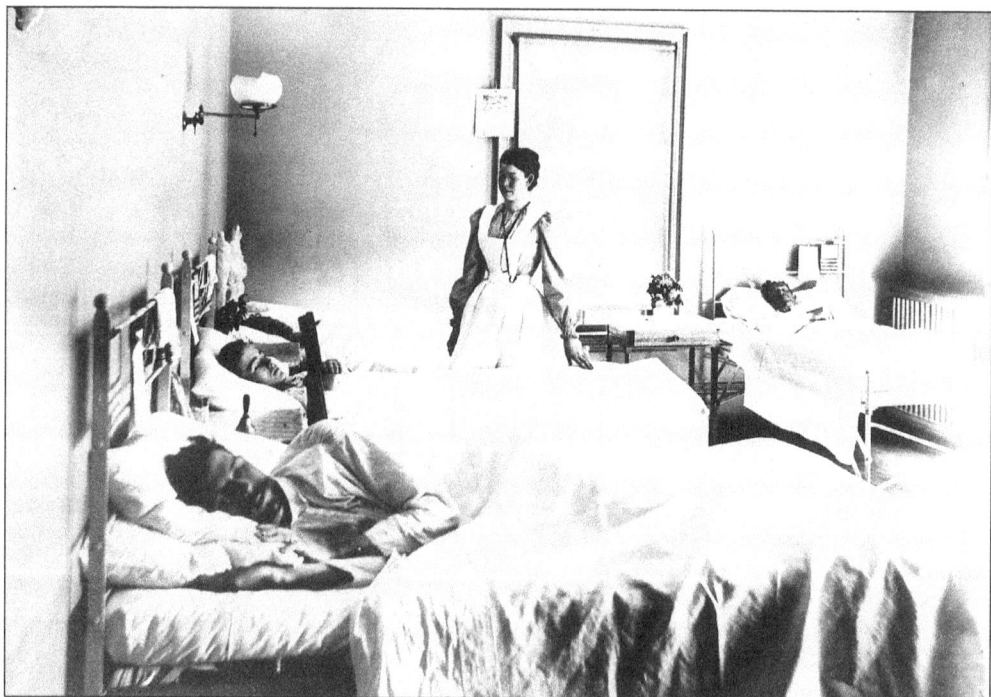

The Male Ward, City Hospital, 1897. Space was at a premium as the hospital tried to keep up with the city's exploding population. A new hospital was built on Buttonwoods Avenue in 1901. The original hospital building was torn down in 1931. (George photograph.)

Dr. Arthur P. George, while an Intern at the City Hospital in 1897. Dr. George (1868–1960) was born in Hampstead, NH, and came to Haverhill after Dartmouth Medical School to become the house officer at the new hospital. His sons, Drs. Alden and Arnold George, followed him in this profession. Arthur George was also an enthusiastic photographer.

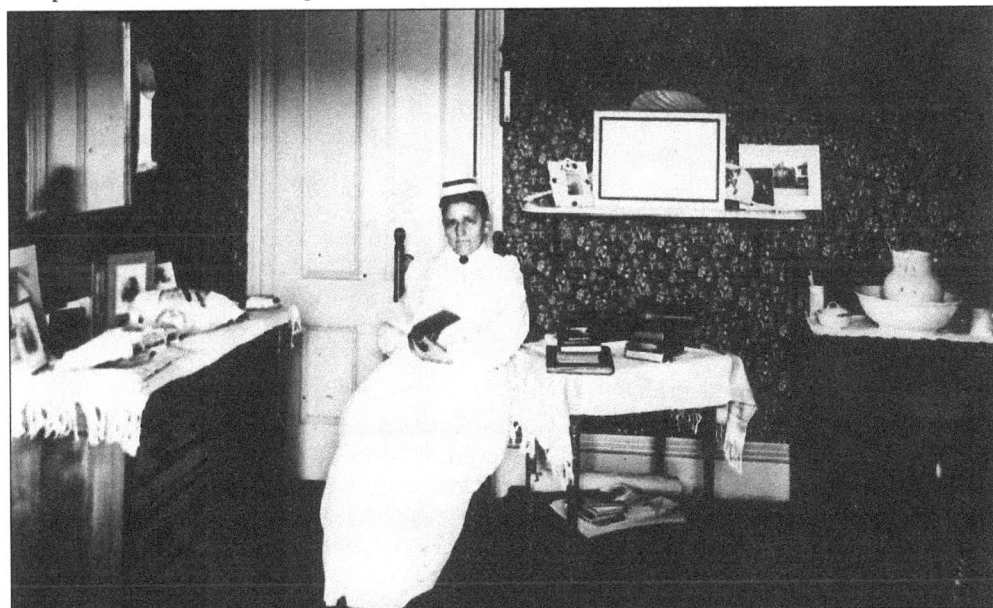

Nurses' Living Quarters, City Hospital, 1897. To become a nurse in the late nineteenth century was not dissimilar to entering a religious life. Nurses were expected to live in their restricted quarters, be on constant call, and lead a virtuous life. Marriage often meant the end of a career. (George photograph.)

Ezekiel James Madison Hale (1813–1881), Haverhill's Most Renowned Philanthropist. A native of Haverhill—a rarity among those featured in this book—Hale had prepared at Bradford Academy and Dartmouth for the practice of law. He chose, instead, to enter the business world, taking over his father's textile factory at Little River. Over time he added more mills, including a large one in South Groveland. His enduring fame, however, rests with his charities. He donated land and money for a Catholic church in South Groveland, and had built an Episcopal church in Groveland. His substantial bequests funded both the new hospital and the new library in Haverhill. He generously supported the Female Benevolent Society and gifted the city with its monument to Hannah Duston. The city has rarely seen a benefactor like Mr. Hale.

The Original Haverhill Public Library. The library was completed in 1875 on Summer Street at the corner of Stage Street. E. J. M. Hale donated the land and almost $200,000 in gifts and bequests. According to his wishes, the city would cover current expenses but a board of trustees would oversee administration.

Reference and Reading Room, Public Library. A wonderful, open, light space to engage in scholarship. Unfortunately, space needs in the early 1900s required the removal of the balcony and the covering over of the open space to provide more rooms. The busts of great writers and thinkers were a gift from E. J. M. Hale.

Edward Capen (1821–1901), First Librarian of the New Public Library. Capen had come to Haverhill in 1874 from his post at the Boston Public Library, where he had served as first librarian of that distinguished institution. The photo above was taken in 1895 by a staff member. Capen is shown seated in the yard at the back of the library. Stage Street is behind him.

The Reading Club at Its Annual Outing. The public library was but the physical expression of a great interest in intellectual pursuits in late nineteenth-century Haverhill. The Monday Evening Club, The Fortnightly Club, The Papyrus Club, and The Reading Club were some of the organizations formed for intellectual stimulation. The women of The Reading Club (below) enjoy a day's outing at the Black Rocks, Salisbury Beach, about 1895.

The Elizabeth Children's Home, Main Street. The Elizabeth Home was begun as a private charity after the Civil War for orphans, "or homeless and neglected little ones." The house was the gift of the Marsh family in memory of their sister, Elizabeth. It served as an alternative to the municipal "poor farm" on Lincoln Street.

The Old Ladies Home, Main Street. It took twenty years of fund raising by the Ladies Charitable Association of Haverhill to finally raise enough to open this home in 1876. Their intent was to provide a dignified retirement home for elderly ladies without family homes or families to care for them. The home is still in operation under the name of the Stevens-Bennett Home.

The Haverhill Historical Society "Buttonwoods" Museum, 240 Water Street. The historical society was founded in 1897 to preserve, protect, and interpret the city's past. The society was given the Samuel Duncan House in 1904 to serve as a museum for its collections. The original part of the house dates from 1814. The terracing, wrap-around veranda, and porte-cochiere were added to the house in the 1880s.

Judge Ira A. Abbott (1845–1921). Judge Abbott was a founder and first president of the Haverhill Historical Society. Abbott, a native of Vermont and a Dartmouth graduate, was a district court judge in Haverhill. From 1905 to 1912, by appointment of President Theodore Roosevelt, he was associate justice of the Supreme Court for the Territory of New Mexico. He returned to Haverhill in 1912 and spent his last years overseeing his numerous realty holdings, and engaging in philanthropic work.

The Kitchen of the John Greenleaf Whittier Birthplace, Amesbury Road. Whittier, one of America's most beloved poets, died on September 6, 1892. Soon after, his birthplace was acquired by the Whittier Club, which had been established in 1886, and it was turned into an historic house museum. The birthplace was first opened to the public one year later on October 12, 1893. Obed Rice Fowler, an artist, whose painting of Whittier's poem *Snowbound* is owned by the library, is shown seated in the kitchen of the birthplace, the setting for that familiar poem.

Whittier Birthplace, August 1895. At this time, the birthplace hosted a gathering of the Haverhill Commandery, #14, Knights Templars, a Masonic group. The house had been in the Whittier family since 1688 until 1836 when the poet sold it. The large central chimney, steep pitched roof, and asymmetrical windows mark it as a Post-Medieval, or First Period, style. It began with four rooms, two down and two up. Later, a kitchen and additional second floor rooms were added, all connected to the large central chimney.

Statue of Hannah Duston, at City Hall Park, Formerly the Haverhill Common, Now the G.A.R. Park. The statue was a gift of E. J. M. Hale. Duston, Haverhill's most well-known woman, was captured by French-led Indians in 1697 during King William's War. She was given into the care of a group of Catholic Indians who had been converted by French priests. It was these Indians, and not those who captured her, that she killed, and later returned to scalp for bounty money. The deed brought her fame in Puritan New England, which cared for neither Indians, nor French, nor Catholics.

Tilton's Tower, on Silver Hill, near the Tilton School. This was Haverhill's most prominent landmark in the late nineteenth and early twentieth century. John C. Tilton (1816–1897), born in West Newbury and a prominent shoe manufacturer, was also actively engaged in land development, especially in the "Mount" Washington area. This 125-foot tower was built in 1887 on his "country estate." His "town house" was on Winter Street at the corner of White Street. The tower was dynamited into rubble soon after World War II when it was replaced by a radio tower.

Seven

City Services

Haverhill's City Hall. The first city government was elected in 1869 and it took office in 1870. Both the form and the powers of government changed with that election, and the political leaders set out to take full advantage of their new status in order to provide a wide array of municipal services to the citizens of Haverhill. The town hall, built in 1861, proved more than sufficient to house the new government. The above photograph was taken in May 1898. Mayor Daniel S. Chase is shown addressing Company F, 8th Regiment of the Massachusetts Volunteer Militia, as it prepares to depart to serve during the Spanish-American War. The photograph, by Lot McNamara, shows clearly the great size and Italianate grandeur of City Hall.

Haverhill Fire Department on Parade. Fire protection in Haverhill had long been on a volunteer basis. The new, growing city required a full-time, paid fire department with stations throughout the city. These are the members of Company 2, looking splendid in their fire helmets, turning onto Merrimack Street from Main Street during a Memorial Day parade in the late 1880s.

Members of Engine and Hose Company E Pose for a Formal Portrait. From left to right they are:(front) H. J. Buck (driver), T. P. Conley (ex-captain), O. A. Smith (lieutenant), W. H. Thomas (engineer), and W. Beardsley (clerk); (back) G. A. Osgood, L. A. Perkins, J. W. Kirby, G. W. Thompson, L. L. Goldsmith (driver), C. H. Follansbee, and G. H. Pulsifer (assistant engineer).

Alden M. Worcester, City Marshall (1850–1925). Haverhill's police department, like the fire department, grew to meet the needs of the city. The department was headed by a marshall, appointed at the will of the mayor and city council. There was no civil service to protect tenure in office. Worcester, a native of Maine, had been a lumberjack in his home state and a heeler in the Haverhill shoe factories. He entered the police force in 1881 and was rapidly promoted to sergeant and captain. He served as Marshall from 1895 to 1900, when this photograph was probably taken, and again from 1919 to 1923.

Patrol Wagon, Haverhill Police Department. The well-equipped police department included a number of these closed wagons, derisively referred to as "paddy wagons," or "Black Mariahs." They were used for transporting law breakers. The policeman has not been identified.

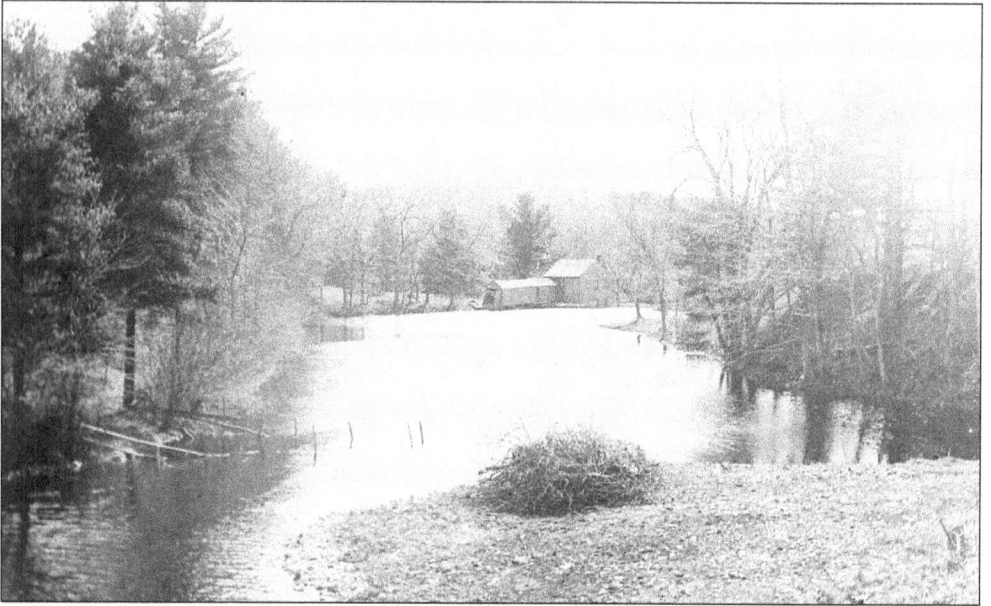

Millvale Pound in the East Parish. The rapid growth of industrial Haverhill required additional water sources. Under the old town government, water services had been supplied by private companies. City government made water supply a municipal service. The Millvale Pond off East Broadway was chosen to be turned into a reservoir to supplement Kenoza Lake and Round Pond.

Dam Construction. Work began in spring 1895 on the dam to control the flow of water from Millvale Pond through Millvale Creek to the Merrimack River. An additional 47 acres of land in the area had to be excavated for the new reservoir. The construction job went to an Italian contractor from New York. The photograph above shows the work in progress by July 1895.

The Italian Workers Camp at Millvale. Over one hundred men, most of them recent immigrants from Italy, arrived to begin the manual excavation of the site. They set up "camp"—in the most accurate sense of the word—and settled in to work.

Italian Workers' Families, Millvale. The workers brought their families with them to take care of their meals and laundry, and to provide a semblance of home life. This was a regular routine for these families. When they finished in Haverhill in November 1895, they moved on to New York for a similar job. The local newspapers considered the workers and their families newsworthy and ran stories on a regular basis about their daily routines, food habits, and living accommodations.

Street Sprinkling Was Another Municipal Service. Although most downtown streets were covered with cobble stones or paving blocks, dust was a perennial problem. As were the ever-visible reminders of the presence of horses on the streets! The street sprinkler is shown beside City Hall Park—the old Common—which had been graded and fenced in 1872 after Haverhill became a city.

The Old Water Pumping Station, Kenoza Lake. The buildings in the foreground were the offices and pumping station of the private Haverhill Aqueduct Co. It had been incorporated as far back as 1802 to provide water to residents in Haverhill. The city purchased the company in 1892. The building on the hill in the background is the original City Hospital. The children with skates and sled, and the upturned rowboats on shore, are a reminder that Kenoza has been a great source of pleasure, as well as the provider of a service. (Bailey photograph, c. 1890)

School Days, School Days. There is probably no aspect of life in the late nineteenth century that so felt the impact of Haverhill's new municipal status as education. Old one-room schoolhouses and wooden neighborhood schools were augmented or replaced by large red brick structures, built to last. Many of them are still in use either as schools or remodeled for housing. Above are some of the children of the Ayers Village School in 1897. Their teacher, Alice Marble, was leaving and they wished to honor her with a party and gifts.

The Gile Street School, near the Plaistow line, 1881. This picture was taken when little girls still wore pinafores to keep their dresses clean. This was a rural one-room school with the traditional two entrances—one for boys and one for girls.

The Thomas E. Burnham School, Fountain St, was built in 1890 and named for the incumbent mayor. The name is indicative of a new trend, to name a school for an individual, rather than for its location. The Burnham School is still in operation.

Thomas E. Burnham (1850–1897), born in West Newbury, came to Haverhill as a child. His widowed mother rented the Duncan "Buttonwoods" House as their home. He was a partner in the Bennett Shoe Co. (see p. 72) and had a distinguished career in city government. He was a member of the Council and of the School Board in the 1880s, and was elected Mayor for three consecutive terms, 1890-93, and asked to fill out an unexpired fourth term. Burnham was mayor during Haverhill's acclaimed 250th anniversary. He died of typhoid fever when he was forty-seven.

Dr. John Crowell, MD (1828–1890). Dr. Crowell was a rarity—a native of Haverhill born at the family home on Water Street. An involved citizen, he served for years as the unpaid chairman of the board of health, trustee of the hospital, of Bradford Academy, and of Linwood Cemetery. He also gave a great number of years of service to the Centre Church as deacon and Sunday school teacher. He was a great admirer of Charles Dickens and was said to resemble him—which explains his pose in this picture.

The Dr. John Crowell School. Located on Belmont Street in the Riverside section, this school was built in 1891 and named for the distinguished citizen who had spent his childhood in that area and had died just the previous year. The Crowell School is still in operation.

The Currier Square School on Washington Street. The mansard roof dates this school to the post-Civil War era when much of this part of town was just beginning to be developed. The photo is by Thomas Bailey and was taken in 1890 for a 250th anniversary publication.

Classroom, Currier Square School, mid-1890s. By the end of the century, the Currier Square area had become heavily built up with the influx of recent Irish, Italian, and Jewish immigrants. The folded hands, straight backs, eyes-straight-ahead deportment of the children would make a parochial school nun feel right at home, as would the crowded classroom.

School Street School, 1890. Built in 1856, this is one of Haverhill's oldest surviving schools. It was also one of the earliest brick ones. Dr. John Crowell served as its first principal, in an interlude from his medical work. The building continued to serve neighborhood children until the latter part of the twentieth century when Haverhill's first new schools since World War I were built. The building has been rehabilitated as apartments. (Bailey photograph.)

Children at the School Street School, c. 1880. Forty-one children, one teacher! The School Street area is where many of the post-Civil War African-American families settled after leaving Virginia and coming to Haverhill.

Championship Baseball Team of the Walnut Square School. The young lads pose with their coach (or he could be the principal?) along with the team mascot, equipment, banners, and prized trophy.

The Walnut Square School. This school on Upper Main Street was designed by architect C. Willis Damon and built in 1899 for the rapidly growing "Avenues" and Highlandville areas. The school was crowded on the day it opened, despite its size. The school is still in operation. This will once again be true of the great E. Howard clock in the tower, which has been silent since 1961.

106

Winter Street School, 1890. This school, built in 1856, served the needs of Yankee, Irish, and French-Canadian families in the old Ward Three area. By the turn of the century, they would be joined by newly arrived Greek families. Saint James Church and the old Saint James Rectory are to the east. The old building is still in use. Today it serves as the Career Resources Center.

Winter Street School Students. One student, Edward Law, (back row, right) has been identified. The names of the others are lost in time. Plaid was a very popular choice for female clothing in the late 1880s, which helps to date this picture to that time period.

Haverhill High School Class in the 1890s. These serious, formally dressed young men and women could almost be law or medical students. Instead, they are Haverhill teenagers attending class at the "new," or Crescent Place, high school. Note the African-American female in the back row. She may be Susie Webster, class of 1892, the first black student to graduate from the school, or she could be Sarah J. Bly, who graduated in 1894.

Linwood O. Towne. Mr. Towne was the chemistry teacher at Haverhill High School in the 1890s and he was later sub-master of the school. In 1899, the City Directory lists him as rooming at 21 Newcomb Street, a few minutes walk from the school.

Class Play, Haverhill High School, 1898. Here is one high school tradition that has endured. The stage at the school auditorium was small and shallow with hardly enough room for the seven actors.

The 1890 Haverhill High School Football Team, second ever at the school. From left to right are: (front) Arthur Hobson (manager) Harry Collins, James Horne (with football; center, coach, and submaster), Thomas Foster, Maurice LeBosquet (see p. 12), and Samuel Duncan (whose home became the Pentucket Club, see p. 13); (back) William McBain, Howard Gordon, John Pollard (he and McBain became doctors), Fred Chase, George Lewis (captain), and Albert Johnson ("first to throw a curve ball in Haverhill High School.")

Track Team of 1890, Complete with Goat for a Mascot. Team members were identified only by last name on the original photograph. They are: (front) Nichols and Corson; (middle) Dean and Peaslee; (back) Savage, Smith, McCarthy, Kimball, Daniels, Jordan, George, Harris, and Brackett.

Haverhill High School Football Team, c. 1899. The team is shown practicing in front of the high school. The quarterback was Jack McCarthy who went on to star at Dartmouth and then became a doctor. The fullback was Joe Lee Jr., the star of the team, and one of Haverhill's greatest all-around athletes. Lee was offered a scholarship to join McCarthy at Dartmouth, but turned it down to get married.

110

The 1898 High School Baseball Team. Joe Lee Jr. (second left in the back row) played center field. To his right is Jack McCarthy, who transferred from Bradford High School, after Bradford was annexed to Haverhill, to pitch for the high school team.

Haverhill High School Track Team of 1899. The first person in the last row is F. Howard Lahey, who would become a world-renowned physician. His teammates, with their future titles in parentheses, include: (front) William Kerrigan, (Dr.) Jack McCarthy, Forrest Smith, David Fitzgerald, Hollis Goodwin; (middle) Bartlett Whittemore, (Dr.) Howard Jewett, Stanley Foster, (Dr.) Ernest Fountaine, Howard Howe; (back) (Dr.) Frank Lahey, William Tuck Jr., Joe Lee Jr., Merrill Luce, Fred J. Smith.

Captain Merrill, Company B, Haverhill High School Cadets. The strong influence of the recent Civil War is apparent in both the uniform and in the concept of a student cadet corps. Merrill has not been further identified.

Helena Mahoney and School Friends, c. 1895. The future Mrs. Clifton Ellis and her chums stand in front of Rufus Chase's house on Main Street (see p. 57) just around the corner from the high school on Crescent Place.

Eight

Faces and Places

The People of Haverhill. This final chapter focuses on the people of late-nineteenth-century Haverhill. The famous and the obscure are remembered through their photographs. More than any written word, the camera has been able to freeze a moment in time, to keep a child forever young, to give a name to someone who had no special reason to be remembered. Above, Mrs. Ben Hosford of Park Street (see p. 63) takes her children and their friends for a ride in her pony cart. They were photographed in front of Austin Nichols' house and we can assume that he took the photograph.

Thomas Sanders (1839–1911). Haverhill's most well-known businessman in the late nineteenth century, Mr. Sanders financed Alexander Graham Bell while Bell experimented with, and then produced, the telephone. Sanders was born in Salem, MA, where he met Bell. He moved to Haverhill in 1874 to enter the shoe sole business. He is seen here, about 1875, in the middle towards the back, wearing a hat.

The Sanders Family and Friends Celebrate the City's 250th Anniversary. Sanders (seated right center) is shown looking over his shoulder. His son, George (standing) was deaf. Sanders hired Alexander Graham Bell as George's tutor. Thus, the inventor and the investor became acquainted. The group is at the home of Jones Frankle on Arlington Place. An emigrant from Germany, Frankle served in the Civil War and left as a brigadier general. He had an insurance business in Haverhill.

Tom Sanders at Birchbrow, the Family Home. Birchbrow, a twenty-room mansion, stood high on a hill at the eastern end of Lake Saltonstall. It was Haverhill's most elegant house by far. After Sanders' death, his children moved away with only occasional visits home. In 1946, the house, after years of neglect, was razed. There is no legacy of the Sanders wealth left in the city, as there is of E. J. M. Hale; only some photographs of a grandeur that once was.

Charles Bradley Sanders, the Son of Thomas, in the Library of Birchbrow. This is the only known photograph of this room, although many of the other rooms in this mansion have been more than adequately photographed.

Ice Delivery near Chestnut Street. The R. Stuart Chase House (right, center), with its recognizable Gothic Revival pointed arches stood at the corner of Summer Street and Chestnut Street. The ice man wears a rubber "apron" on his back. The ice block would be picked up with tongs and carried on his back to be placed in one of the new tin-lined, wooden ice boxes that were becoming very common in houses. This form of house-to-house, horse-drawn wagon, ice delivery went on right up until the end of World War II, when prosperity made the ice box obsolete. Wherever there was an ice wagon in the summer, there were sure to be children hanging about asking for a sliver of ice to chew on—an early form of a popsicle!

An American Express Wagon and Driver. They are awaiting packages at the northern end of Railroad Square. The office of the American Express was at 113 Washington Street. The poster advertises an open air Gospel Service by or for the Railroad Department. The building behind is the Gardner Block, built in 1872, by S. Porter Gardner (see p. 64) to be the first shoe shop to which newly arrived shoe workers would see and seek employment. Simon Starensier, a Jewish immigrant from Eastern Europe, opened a shoe business here at the end of the century that lasted until modern decades.

The Automobile Age Approaches Haverhill. Thomas Duston, shown here with his sister, built this car himself in 1899, the year the photograph was taken. Along with a new century, the auto age, too, was on the horizon.

Everyone Loves Pictures of Children. On these facing pages are four quite different views. The two children above are Harvey and Arthur Taft Chase, sons of R. Stuart Chase of Summer Street (see p. 116)

Two Youngsters about to Enjoy a Winter's Day of Sledding. They stand in front of 3 White Street at the corner of Winter Street. The handsome wrought iron fence suggests the status of this neighborhood.

Attention! Parade About To Begin! A group of Groveland Street neighborhood children line up for the photographer all ready for a grand parade. The flag, toy rifle, and toy sword seem appropriate, but was the violin intended to replace a brass band?

Immigrant Children on Washington Street at Either Temple or Jackson Street. A significant number of recent Italian and Jewish immigrants lived in this neighborhood. The world of these children shown here was vastly different from those who lived on Summer, White, or Groveland Streets.

Children on the Ice at the Little River Falls. Foolhardiness is not a modern invention, as these children demonstrate in 1900. Ezekiel Hale's factory is on the right off Winter Street.

Albert G. Harding and Family Pose, and Pose Again, for the Photographer. A double-exposure has removed half of Harding's body making him appear like a spectre. On the upper right, one of his younger daughters appears to float behind a large plant. Harding, an insurance agent, lived at 51 North Avenue. Photography could be fun, as this shot demonstrates.

Isaac W. "Ike" Roberts. Born in Liberia, Roberts came to Haverhill when his father became minister of Calvary Baptist Church. He graduated from the high school in 1895, went on to study soil chemistry, and took his knowledge back to Liberia where he became a successful plantation owner and export trader. He was knighted by the President of Liberia for his services to that country.

The Charles LeBosquet Family. The whole group is shown preparing for a bicycle jaunt behind their house at 40 Arlington Street. Helen is at the left rear, with the long braid of hair. Thomas is in the white shirt in front.

Summertime, and the Living Is So Easy! George H. Leighton and his family and friends enjoy a relaxed afternoon in the pine grove at John J. Marsh's, on the left-hand side of North Broadway. What more can one ask for in life?

Sun Porch on the Gilman House. John P. Gilman, a hat manufacturer, built his house about 1860 on 38 Summer Street at Highland Avenue. His widow, Frances Hale Gilman, a sister of E. J. M. Hale, added the sun room in 1880 to the southeast corner. Mrs. Gilman (wearing a hat) is seated on the right while her son reads aloud to her and her daughter. The house was torn down in 1945, as stipulated in Mrs. Gilman's will.

The Great Cast-Iron Stove. Also called the Crawford Range, this was a wonderful multi-purpose device. It could cook the food, heat the kitchen, warm the bath water, provide shelves to cool the baked goods, and, as demonstrated above, did wonders for cold feet on a winter's night. The stove was the practical alternative to the sun room. The man, so comfortably ensconced by the stove, is probably John Plummer, 140 North Avenue, a foreman in a shoe shop.

Seth Bassett with Wife and Friend. Bassett led a rich and full business life ranging from mail clerk to newspaper publisher, but he was known best for the tours he organized. At first he took annual trips to the White Mountains with students from Bradford Academy and from other select schools. In time, he expanded both his locales and his audience, personally guiding tours as far away as Florida, Alaska, and Hawaii. Bassett died in 1930, but his widow, Lillian, continued the business. (Nichols photograph.)

Lydia G. Bailey, of 30 Park Street. The wife of Thomas Bailey, druggist and photographer, poses on the graceful curving staircase in her Victorian home. The decor is rich with patterns: wallpaper, carpets, rugs, upholstery. The gas lamp on the newel post has been re-fitted for electricity. (Bailey photograph, c. 1895.)

Mrs. Thomas Bailey Sways in the Hammock, while her friend, Ida Clay, rocks away a hot summer's day at the Bailey house, 30 Park Street. (Bailey photograph, *c.* 1900)

Family of Walter Scott Leighton, a Carpenter. This family had neither sun room nor hammocks. They just sat on the front stoop of their home on Gile Street when it became too hot. Shown are Walter (center), and his wife (upper left), along with their three daughters, Walter's sister Grace (by the door), and her husband, Almon Riley (left).

Christmas at the Dudley Porter Home, Corner of Maple Avenue and Park Street. Porter (1837–1905), was a shoe manufacturer, banker, library trustee, and park commissioner. He was reputed to have one of the best private libraries in New England. On the day of his funeral, public schools and City Hall offices were closed. Many retail businesses and factories closed during the hour of his funeral service and burial.

Sam Wilson, Hack Driver. Wilson conducted a delivery service from his office in Bradford. He is shown here, with his hack or taxi, waiting for customers in Railroad Square. He is in front of the Carleton Block on Wingate Street.

Mrs. Melissa Cromwell, Milliner. Mrs. Cromwell designed and created women's hats in her store at 174 Merrimack Street. She did not own a house, but rented rooms near her business. No schools, factories, nor city government offices were closed on the day of Mrs. Cromwell's funeral, nor of that of Sam Wilson, hack driver. (Photograph c. 1895.)

Blind Man Selling Pencils in Washington Square, *c.* 1895. The man sits in front of the "new" post office. His name is no longer known, but old-timers remember hearing about him. The building across the square at the corner of Emerson Street was built in 1860 by developer Franklin Brickett. He also built the Franklin Block on the opposite corner on Merrimack Street. They are the two oldest brick buildings at that end of town. The Brickett name was removed and replaced by that of Clarence Coombs when he bought the building. Barely visible to the left rear is the Carbone Bros. Fruit Store, begun about 1890 by Michael Carbone and his five brothers. They were among the earliest immigrants to Haverhill from Italy. The Carbone family had a store in this location until 1953. The Washington Square area survived Urban Renewal and became one of the first beneficiaries, along with Washington Street, of the historic preservation movement. Thus, an integral part of Haverhill's nineteenth-century past has been protected for the future.

Visit us at
arcadiapublishing.com

www.ingramcontent.com/pod-product-compliance
Lightning Source LLC
Chambersburg PA
CBHW080858100426
42812CB00007B/2072